A World of and Fantasy

Coloring Book

By Molly Harrison

www.mollyharrisonart.com

From the Artist

Thank you for purchasing my coloring book A World of Fairies and Fantasy!

Please be sure to put a couple pieces of paper
or a piece of cardstock between the pages
if coloring with markers to prevent bleed through.

Find PDF printable coloring books in my Etsy shop
etsy.com/shop/mollyharrisonart
and
mollyharrisonart.com

Find me on Patreon where you can subscribe and
receive monthly coloring pages and more!
patreon.com/fantasyartistmolly